HOW TO MAKE A
RAINBOW

For readers and young scientists
of every color!

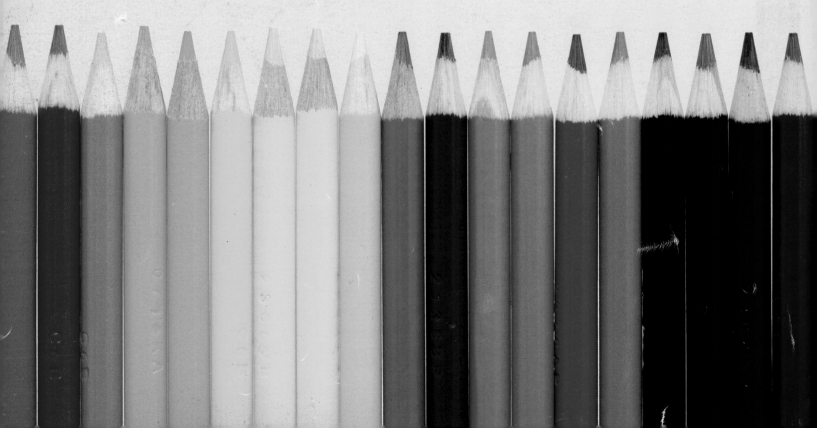

HOW TO
MAKE A
RAINBOW

A CRAYOLA COLOR STORY

LAURA PURDIE SALAS

M MILLBROOK PRESS • MINNEAPOLIS

© 2018 Crayola, Easton, PA 18044-0431. Crayola Oval Logo, Serpentine Design, Wild Watermelon, Sunset Orange, Banana Mania, Inchworm, Screamin' Green, Granny Smith Apple, Blue Bell, Purple Mountains' Majesty, and Purple Heart are registered trademarks of Crayola and used under license.

Official Licensed Product
Millbrook Press
A division of Lerner Publishing Group, Inc.
241 First Avenue North
Minneapolis, MN 55401 USA

For reading levels and more information, look up this title at www.lernerbooks.com.

Main body text set in Billy Infant Regular 15/20. Typeface provided by SparkyType.

Library of Congress Cataloging-in-Publication Data

Names: Salas, Laura Purdie, author.
Title: How to make a rainbow : a Crayola color story / by Laura Purdie Salas.
Description: Minneapolis : Millbrook Press, 2018. | Includes bibliographical references. | Audience: Ages 4-9. | Audience: K to Grade 3.
Identifiers: LCCN 2017006351 (print) | LCCN 2017018949 (ebook) | ISBN 9781512498677 (eb pdf) | ISBN 9781512439922 (lb : alk. paper)
Subjects: LCSH: Rainbows—Juvenile literature. | Color—Juvenile literature.
Classification: LCC QC976.R2 (ebook) | LCC QC976.R2 .S25 2018 (print) | DDC 535.6—dc23

LC record available at https://lccn.loc.gov/2017006351

Manufactured in the United States of America
1-42254-26119-8/8/2017

TABLE OF CONTENTS

INTRODUCTION

Welcome, young scientists. Won't you join today's experiment? We're going to make a rainbow.

What's a rainbow?

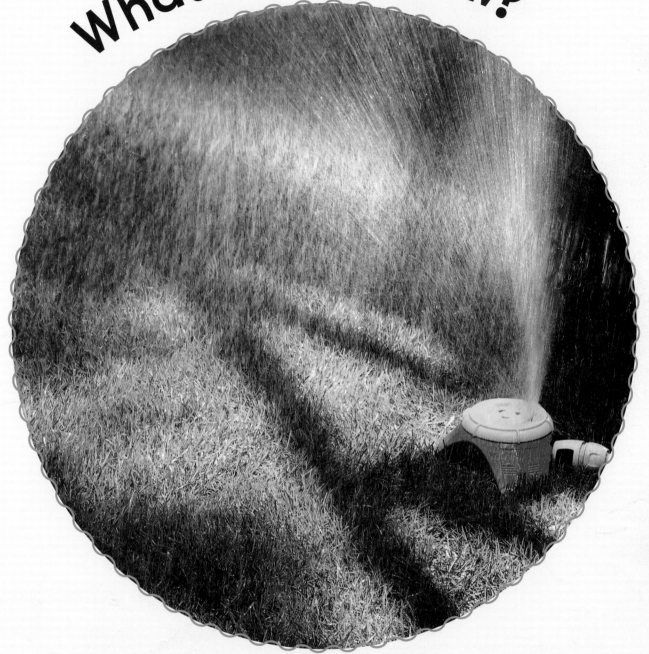

Why, it's a fantastic display of dazzling colors.

A parade of shades!

A view of hues!

The sky is your laboratory. The rain has stopped, and the air is still damp. To make a rainbow, you just need to add sunshine. And the sun is about to peek out from behind those clouds. Perfect! Can you predict what will happen next?

Colors!

Which colors do you see?

What You Need to Make a Rainbow

moist air

sunshine

RED

Ready?

Let's start with reds!

vroom!

ruby

apple for your teacher

cardinal

STOP

ORANGE

Orange you smart to find so much orange!

fall leaves

orange—that one was easy!

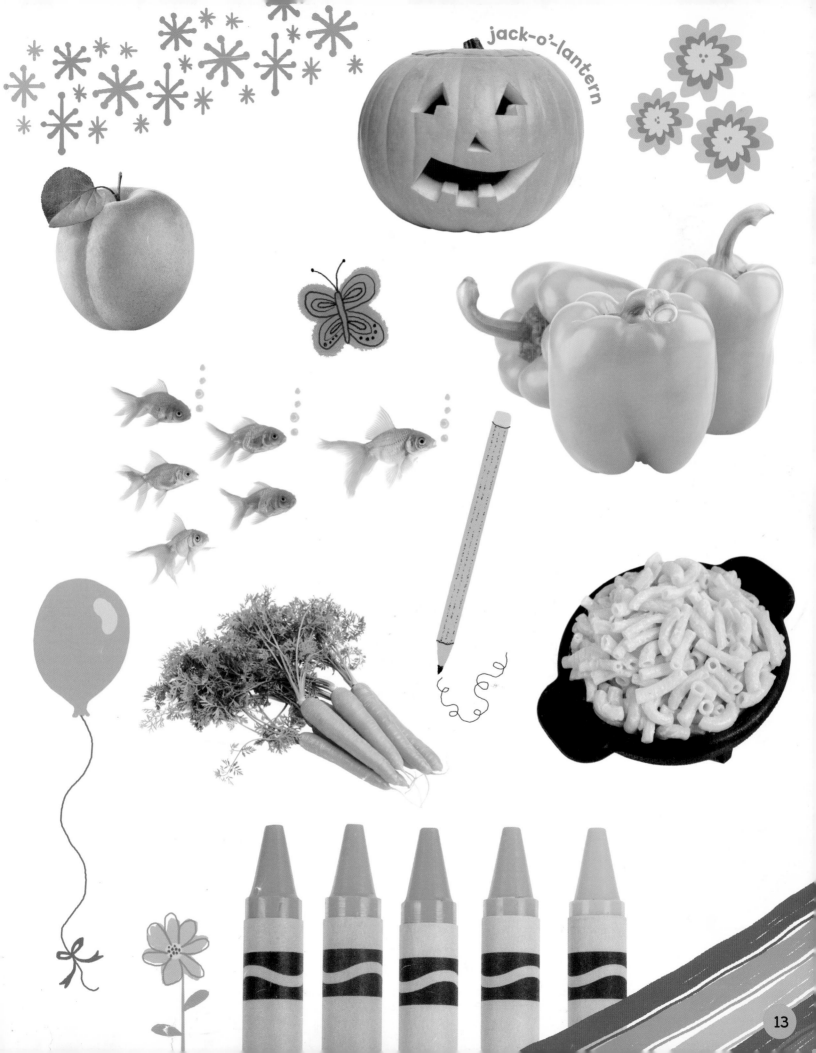

jack-o'-lantern

YELLOW

Amazing yellows brighten up your laboratory.

goldenrod

rubber duckies

lemonade–*ahhhhh!*

canary

GREEN

Great gobs of green!
Look what you've found!

inchworm

shamrocks

parrot—squawk!

frog—there it goes!

mint chocolate
chip ice cream

BLUE

Ah, blue. Blue is truly, bluely everywhere!

turquoise

blue morpho butterfly

oceans

blue tang

blue lobster
(rare but real!)

INDIGO

Indigo. Now here's a color name we don't say often. Indigo is dark blue with a little hint of purple. Can you find indigo hiding in the world?

Blue Angels jet

indigo bunting

purple emperor—should be called an indigo emperor!

bluebottle fly

blue milk mushroom

indigo plant

VIOLET

And your very last color—vivid violet!

purple starling

wisteria

orchid

violets

You are amazing! Look at all these colors you've found. But without any order, they're just . . .

colors.

In our experiment, the colors came in order. When sunlight bounces off tiny, curved water droplets, it bends and arranges itself into a fine design of colored lines from red to orange to yellow to green to blue to indigo to violet. That's what changes just colors into . . .

. . . a rainbow!

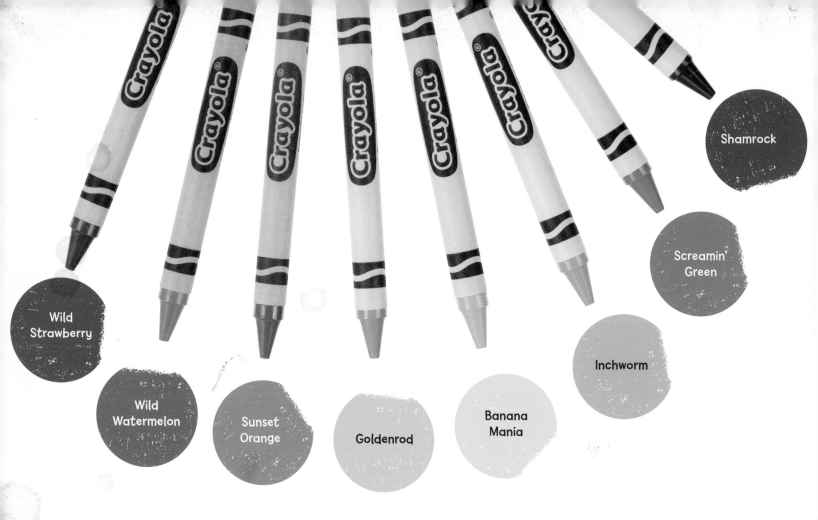

Shamrock

Screamin' Green

Inchworm

Wild Strawberry

Wild Watermelon

Sunset Orange

Goldenrod

Banana Mania

WORLD OF COLORS

Our world is full of beautiful colors. Here are some of the Crayola®
crayons used in this book. Can you find them in the photos?

Cornflower Blue

Blue Bell

Sky Blue

Navy Blue

Robin's Egg Blue

Purple Mountains' Majesty

Granny Smith Apple

Purple Heart

MAKE A RAINBOW

You can make your own rainbow! Using materials you can find at home or at school, create a rainbow that you can hang wherever you need a little extra color.

What You Need

coffee filter

scissors

plastic trash bag

3 plastic cups

water

red, yellow, and blue food dye

something to stir with

paintbrush

glue

cotton balls

How to Make Your Rainbow

1. Fold a coffee filter in half. With an adult's help, cut a small half circle out of the straight side so your filter has a curved rainbow shape. Keep both halves of the filter together for the whole project.

2. Cover your workspace with a plastic trash bag. Lay your filter flat on the bag.

3. Fill all three cups with about 1 inch (2.5 cm) of water. Add 10 drops of one dye to each cup. Stir in the dye.

4. Paint a red stripe along the top of the rainbow-shaped filter. Dab on more color, and watch it spread downward a little.

5. Paint a yellow stripe in the middle of the rainbow. Blend the edges of the yellow and red stripes to make an orange stripe.

6. Paint a blue stripe at the bottom of the rainbow. Blend the edges of the yellow and blue stripes to make a green stripe. Blend a bit of red with the very bottom of the blue stripe to make a violet stripe.

7. Let your rainbow dry.

8. Glue cotton balls at both ends to make clouds.

GLOSSARY

blend: to shade into each other

damp: slightly wet

design: a pattern

hue: a color, or a shade of a color

laboratory: a room or building that has special equipment for people to use in scientific experiments

material: an item you need for a project or activity

moist: slightly wet

TO LEARN MORE

Books

McKee, David. *Elmer and the Rainbow*. Minneapolis: Andersen, 2011.
A rainbow has lost its colors! Find out what happens in this story when Elmer the elephant decides to give his colors to the rainbow.

Nelson, Robin. *From Wax to Crayon*. Minneapolis: Lerner Publications, 2013.
Read this book to learn how a crayon gets made.

Sweeney, Monica. *How the Crayons Saved the Rainbow*. New York: Sky Pony, 2016.
Join a box of crayons on their adventure to bring color back to a rainbow!

Websites

Color Spinners
http://www.crayola.com/crafts/color-spinners-craft/
This color spinner craft project can help you make even more rainbows appear.

Why Do Rainbows Appear?
http://wonderopolis.org/wonder/why-do-rainbows-appear
Visit this website to learn more about rainbows and to try some fun activities!

PHOTO ACKNOWLEDGMENTS

The images in this book are used with the permission of: Chiyacat/Shutterstock, p. 5 (sandals); FamVeld/Shutterstock, p. 6; iStock/vm, p. 7; Dmitry Pichugin/Shutterstock, pp. 8-9; Christoff/ Shutterstock, p. 10 (car); iStock/skodonnell, p. 10 (fire truck); iStock/FGorgun, p. 10 (bricks); iStock/ Zelfit, p. 10 (ruby); JeniFoto/Shutterstock, pp. 10, 11, 27 (cookies); Tim UR/Shutterstock, pp. 10 (apple), 12 (orange); p. 26 (red apple); Diana Taliun/Shutterstock, p. 11 (tulips); Valentina Razumova/ Shutterstock, pp. 11, 26 (strawberry); Dmitrij Skorobogatov/Shutterstock, pp. 11, 27 (grapefruit); Timolina/ Shutterstock, p. 11 (watermelon); Maks Narodenko/Shutterstock, pp. 11 (tomato), 16 (apples), 24 (tomato), 26 (green apples), 27 (tomato); Charles Brutlag/Shutterstock, pp. 11, 25 (cardinal); Kaspri/Shutterstock, p. 11 (stop sign); Aleksandr Bryliaev/Shutterstock, p. 11 (gloves); niwat chaiyawoot/Shutterstock, pp. 12, 26 (basketball); HorenkO/Shutterstock, pp. 12, 26 (maple leaf); pryzmat/Shutterstock, p. 12 (cones); Butterfly Hunter/Shutterstock, p. 12 (butterfly); © Catzovescu/Dreamstime, pp. 13, 24, 27 (pumpkin); Palokha Tetiana/ Shutterstock, pp. 13, 27 (apricot); EM Arts/Shutterstock, p. 13 (peppers); S-F/Shutterstock, p. 13 (goldfish); LorenzoArcobasso/Shutterstock, pp. 13, 27 (carrots); © Matt Antonino/Dreamstime, p. 13 (mac & cheese); iStock/ DigtialStorm, p. 14 (bus); Africa Studio/Shutterstock, p. 14 (ducklings); Tish1/Shutterstock, pp. 14, 26 (rubber ducks); iStock/Chushkin, p. 14 (goldenrod); vilax/Shutterstock, pp. 14-15, 26, 32 (dandelions); Egor Rodynchenko/ Shutterstock, pp. 15, 25, 27 (bananas); Igor Polyakov/Shutterstock, pp. 15, 27 (lemon); © Unknown1861/ Dreamstime, p. 15 (lemonade); Eric Isselee/Shutterstock, pp. 15 (canary) (puppy), 20 (peacock), 24 (canary); iStock/arlindo71, pp. 16, 26 (worm); turtix/Shutterstock, pp. 16, 24 (lime); HABRDA/Shutterstock, pp. 16, 26 (shamrocks); iStock/bluecinema, p. 16 (olives); Tracy Starr/Shutterstock, p. 17 (parrot); iStock/aluxum, pp. 17, 27 (frog); Anna Kucherova/Shutterstock, p. 17 (avocado); kao/Shutterstock, p. 17 (leaf); iStock/Scovad, p. 17 (tree); zcw/Shutterstock, pp. 17, 25, 27 (asparagus); lendy16/Shutterstock, pp. 17, 24, 27 (money); Charles Brutlag/ Shutterstock, p. 17 (ice cream); Keith Homan/Shutterstock, p. 18 (nest); Le Do/Shutterstock, pp. 18, 21, 25, 27 (flowers); iStock/LVV, pp. 18, 26 (turquoise); Marc Bruxelle/Shutterstock, pp. 18, 26 (Blue Morpho butterfly); Double Brow Imagery/Shutterstock, p. 18 (bluebird); Scisetti Alfio/Shutterstock, p. 19 (coneflowers); © Abidal/ Dreamstime, pp. 19, 25 (earth); Mike Flippo/Shutterstock, pp. 19, 27 (ribbon); iStock/TomekD76, pp. 19, 25, 27 (lobster); bluehand/Shutterstock, p. 19 (fish); ifong/Shutterstock, pp. 19, 27 (blueberries); iStock/KGrif, pp. 20, 26 (jet); marylooo/Shutterstock, p. 20 (jeans); JewelStudio/Shutterstock, pp. 20, 26 (lapis); Dan Thornberg/ Shutterstock, p. 20 (flag); Jack Jeffrey/BIA/Minden Pictures/Getty Images, p. 21 (bird); Mark Johnson/ Westend61/Newscom, pp. 21, 24, 26 (Purple Emperor butterfly); iStock/sirichai_raksue, p. 21 (fly); Rich Graessle/ Icon Sportswire/Newscom, p. 21 (helmet); Dan Molter/Wikimedia Commons (CC BY-SA 3.0), p. 21 (mushroom); Anna Kucherova/Shutterstock, pp. 22, 26 (eggplant); MrBright/Shutterstock, p. 22 (amethyst); Karkas/Shutterstock, pp. 22, 26 (shoes); iStock/eli_asenova, pp. 22, 25 (plums); iStock/APPOLLOMAN, p. 22 (pigeon); Aivar Mikko/Alamy Stock Photo, pp. 22, 24 (starling); homydesign/Shutterstock, pp. 23, 24 (wisteria); Jomwaschara Komvorn/ Shutterstock, p. 23 (orchid); Fotyma/Shutterstock, pp. 23, 24, 27 (starfish); Air Kanlaya/Shutterstock, pp. 23, 27 (cabbage); © Margo555/Dreamstime, pp. 23, 27 (violets); Daina Lockie/Shutterstock, p. 29 (watercolor background); Courtesy Rachel Kaylynn/http://joyfullyweary.blogspot.com/, p. 29 (coffee filter rainbow).

Cover: Superheang168/Shutterstock (watermelon); Charles Brutlag/Shutterstock (cardinal); Suslik1983/ Shutterstock (basketball); Tinnaporn Sathapornnanont/Shutterstock (ducks); kubais/Shutterstock (sunflower); Slavko Sereda/Shutterstock (shamrock); iStock/Olha_stock (frog); Gary C. Tognoni/Shutterstock (nest); pukach/ Shutterstock (balloon); ericlefrancais/Shutterstock (shoes); Butterfly Hunter/Shutterstock (butterfly).